Real-Life Princes

Karen Latchana Kenney

Bumba Books™

LERNER PUBLICATIONS ◆ MINNEAPOLIS

Note to Educators

Throughout this book, you'll find critical-thinking questions. These can be used to engage young readers in thinking critically about the topic and in using the text and photos to do so.

Lerner Publications Company
A division of Lerner Publishing Group, Inc.
241 First Avenue North
Minneapolis, MN 55401 USA

For reading levels and more information, look up this title at www.lernerbooks.com.

Library of Congress Cataloging-in-Publication Data

Names: Kenney, Karen Latchana, author.
Title: Real-life princes / Karen Latchana Kenney.
Description: Minneapolis : Lerner Publications, 2020. | Series: Bumba books. Real-life royalty | Includes bibliographical references and index. | Audience: Age 4–7. | Audience: K to Grade 3.
Identifiers: LCCN 2018044385 (print) | LCCN 2018045998 (ebook) | ISBN 9781541561328 (eb pdf) | ISBN 9781541557284 (lb : alk. paper) | ISBN 9781541561328 (eb pdf)
Subjects: LCSH: Princes—Juvenile literature.
Classification: LCC D412.7 (ebook) | LCC D412.7 .K46 2020 (print) | DDC 940.56/120922—dc23

LC record available at https://lccn.loc.gov/2018044385

Manufactured in the United States of America
1-46143-45748-2/20/2019

Table of Contents

Let's Meet a Prince!

It's a royal parade!

Soldiers march by.

The prince stands up

and salutes them.

Prince William from the United Kingdom

Prince Gabriel
from Belgium

A prince is part of a royal family.

Prince Gabriel's parents are

the king and queen of Belgium.

His sisters are princesses.

His brother is a prince too.

Prince Naruhito lives in Japan.

He will become the leader one day.

He will be the emperor of Japan.

Prince Naruhito from Japan

Some princes live in big homes.

The Prince of Wales lives in London.

A prince may go to big dinners.

Leaders visit from other countries.

Why might a royal family have big dinners?

Prince Charles from the United Kingdom

Prince Harry from the United Kingdom

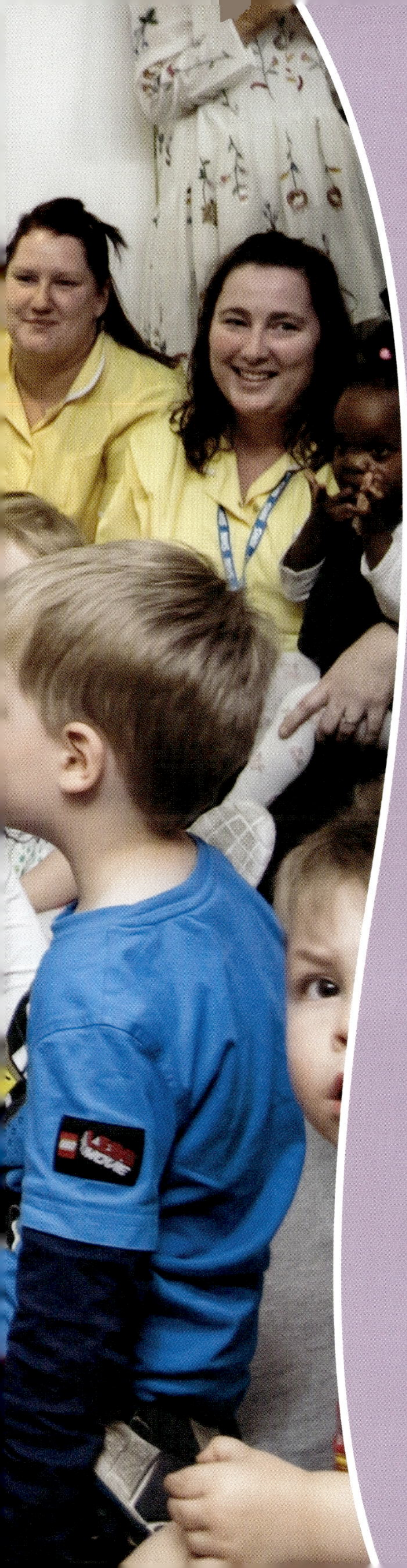

A prince meets his people.

He visits hospitals and schools.

A prince also gives speeches. The prince of Bahrain speaks to world leaders.

What do you think a prince might speak about?

Prince Salman from Bahrain

Prince Frederik from Denmark

Some princes are soldiers.

They serve their country.

Prince Frederik wears his uniform and medals.

A prince learns how to be a king.

One day, he will lead the royal family.

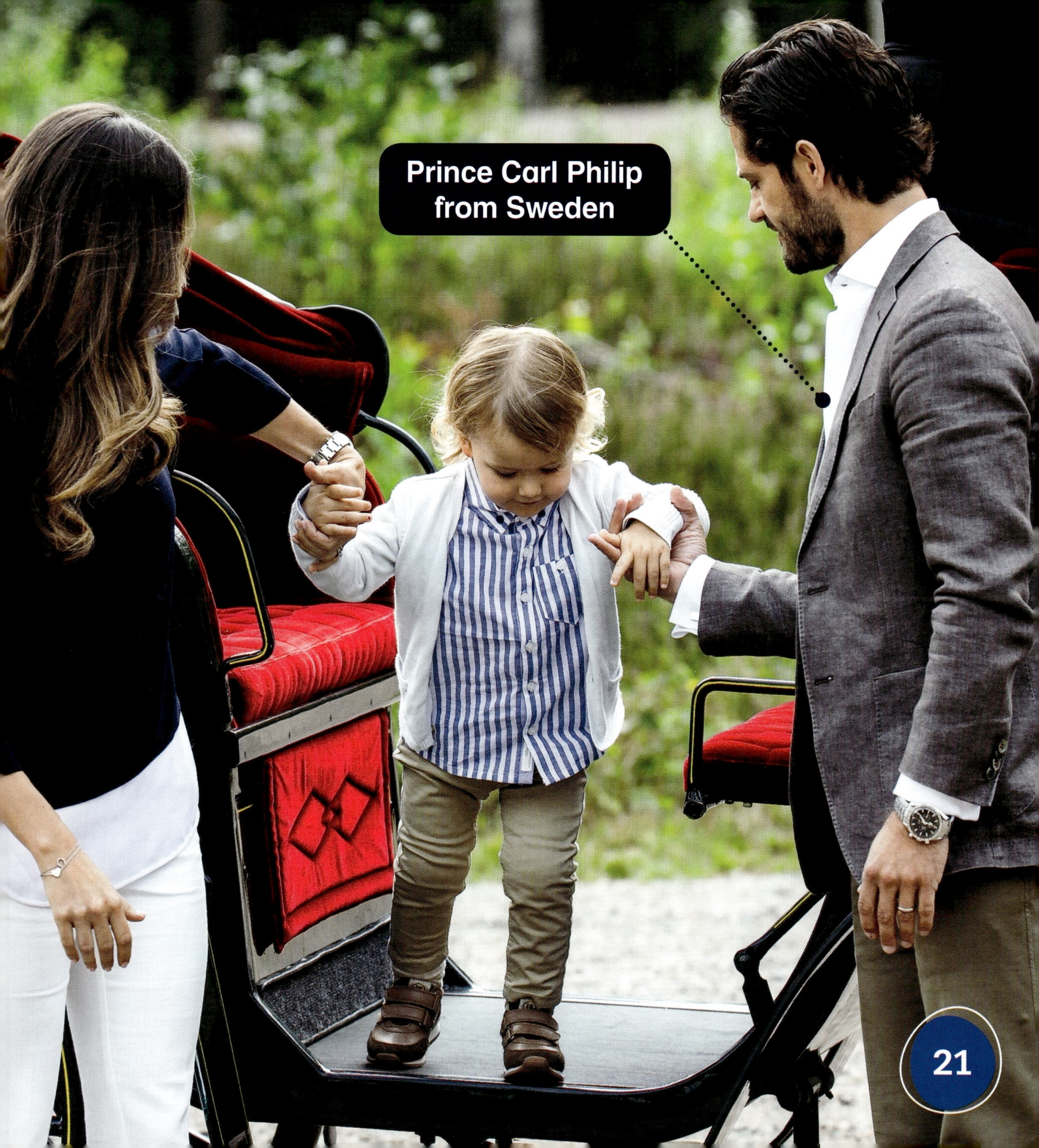
Prince Carl Philip
from Sweden

Life as a Prince

Picture Glossary

emperor

royalty in Japan that is like a king

salutes

raises a hand and arm to show respect

speeches

formal talks in front of a crowd

uniform

clothing worn by all members of a group such as the military

Read More

Kenney, Karen Latchana. *Real-Life Kings.* Minneapolis: Lerner Publications, 2020.

Kenney, Karen Latchana. *Real-Life Princesses.* Minneapolis: Lerner Publications, 2020.

Ribke, Simone T. *William and Kate: The Prince and Princess.* New York: Children's Press, 2016.

Index

Photo Credits

Image credits: Max Mumby/Indigo/Getty Images, pp. 5, 23 (top right); Patrick Aventurier/WireImage/Getty Images, p. 6; Kyodo News/Getty Images, pp. 9, 23 (top left); Chris Jackson/Getty Images, pp. 10, 22 (bottom); Chris Jackson/Getty Images, p. 13; Danny Lawson/WPA Pool/Getty Images, p. 14; Andrew Cowie/AFP/Getty Images, pp. 17, 23 (bottom left); Mark Cuthbert/UK Press/Getty Images, pp. 18, 23 (bottom right); Michael Campanella/WireImage/Getty Images, p. 21; Julian Parker/UK Press/Getty Images, p. 22 (left); Michael Dunlea/Alamy Stock Photo, p. 22 (top).

Cover: Anwar Hussein/WireImage/Getty Images.